Unemployment and Poverty in Rural America

The Life and Hillbilly Culture of the Poor Majority

By Naven Johnson

Table of Contents

Introduction

In the recent years, research has studied the unusual increase in the number of prime aged men who are unemployed. According to Nicholas Eberstadt, a political economist who holds the Henry Wendt Chair in Political Economy at the American Enterprise Institute, the drop of the share of prime aged men in the labor market in other prosperous democracies has never been as severe as in the United States.

Eberstadt tackles the anticipated problem of what unemployed men do during their free time. He highlights the average time they spend in front of the screens is around over 2,000 hours per year which is comparable to a full-time job. Based on this terrifying fact, Eberstadt questions their readiness and abilities if they decide to return to work.

Controversial arguments, based on the presented data and facts, might debate the root cause of the increasing number of prime aged unemployed men. Some arguments might endorse globalization and economic change as the prime root cause but others might as well explore education and disabilities. However, Eberstadt focus on a widely dismissed shocking aspect which is the correlation between the presented phenomena and the crisis of men previously charged with a felony. Different researches have explored the topic from different angles such as psychological and upbringing tragedies, rent-seeking and addiction.

The Mystery of Unemployment

Since 1970, the number of men aged from 25 to 54 who are not working or hunting for a job has doubled. The labor market seems to encompass a steadily shrinking number of men who do not hold a college degree. Compared to all the 35 member states of the Organization for Economic Co-operation and Development (OECD) (with the exception of Italy) as a result of its economic turmoil and Israel which is considered an anomaly as a consequence of Jewish Orthodox men unwilling to work, the integration of prime aged men without a college degree in the labor force in the United States is noticeably lower. Although the United States has a strong economic position compared to the 22 prosperous countries of the OECD, it has ranked 22nd in the participation rate of prime aged men in the labor force. Eberstadt calls this unfortunate situation "the unwelcome American exceptionalism"

Moreover, one out of six American men are either unemployed or unfit for work. This sums up to 10 million American men. The crucial question that should be asked is where the 10 million men go. Various justifications have been proposed to explain the situation. According to a report released by the White House economists, unemployed prime-aged men are not precisely young, and most of them are not parents. They are unreasonably black, less educated, and the majority live in the South.

Furthermore, the situation is alarming because it is constantly increasing without social riots or even debates. Today, even after the economic expansion started in June 2009, the percentage of prime aged men working is smaller than those who were working by the end of the Great Depression back in 1940 when the unemployment rate was greater 14%. If the participation rate in the labor force today were close to the participation rate in 2000, 10 million more Americans would have a job.

Men Without Work

Nicholas Eberstadt explores in his monograph Men Without Work: America's Invisible Crisis the economic and moral reasons behind the 13% decline of the male participation rate in workforce in the last half-century. Men, nowadays, are restructuring the norms and proving that seeking a job can be voluntary. This radical transformation seems to remain invisible to the government because men who chose to remain unemployed are not actually counted as unemployed because they are regarded by the government as if they were hunting for jobs.

Moreover, Eberstadt explains his expression "normative sea change" as the fact that men with the ability to work are choosing to live on their savings or kind donations. Only 15% of men who did not work in 2014 admit they are unemployed because they failed to find a suitable job; this means that the rest are actually choosing to remain unemployed. In the past 50 years, the number of men who are neither working nor seeking jobs has increased 4 times more than the number of those who are working or hunting for jobs. The numbers seem to remain uninfluenced by economic cycles.

Furthermore, the government has admitted the existence of 'economically inactive' men and has discovered they are the main category of jobless men. The number of 'economically inactive' men seem to overcome the number of unemployed men even before government policies and social trends made it feasible to be 'economically inactive'. The rise of this trend is indirectly enforced by benefits and grants provided by the government as well as financial support from family members. Surprisingly, due to such support, 'economically inactive' men spend one third more than workers receiving minimum wage rates. According to Eberstadt, they are more stable economically than millions of Americans especially single mothers who are working or hunting for jobs.

Additionally, the flight of prime aged men from the labor market has been the target of various explanation efforts lately. It has been suggested they might be students, disabled, jailed, or stay at home husbands and fathers. However, investigations based on each suggestion show that none of them fully deciphers the disturbing dilemma.

College and Unemployment

Although this explanation of the increasing number of American men remaining unemployed seems to be harmless and even highly optimistic, it does not effectively untangle the complexity of the situation. In fact, the number of prime aged men continuing their studies beyond secondary education has hardly increased since the 90's from 2.5 million to 3 million. This increase has reflected on the number of men working part time. However, it slightly clarifies the increasing number of unemployed men. If the participation rate of prime aged men in the labor market has remained the same since 1990, there should about 3 million more working men in the labor market than the actual figure.

Today, men fleeing the labor force are most likely the ones who did not get into post-secondary institutes. They are four times more likely to quit the job market than fifty years ago when the high school graduates and college graduates were equally likely to get into the labor force. Nowadays, prime aged men are better educated than back in 1964 which should have paved their path easily to the labor market in which college graduates have a higher participation rate. However, men who did not continue their education past high school are falling out of the job market and that is the real mystery.

How Disability Affects the Workplace

Disability is a very frequent explanation for the fall of male presence in America's workforce. However, it does not totally uncover the mystery of the decreasing number of men in the labor market. In the United States of America, Social Security Disability Insurance or SSDI which is managed by the Social Security Administration, is granted to individuals who cannot be employed because of physical disability. SSDI can, with no doubts, be the motive behind people quitting employment if they prove they cannot work full time. Therefore, SSDI may be criticized as the policy alienates individuals who are capable to contribute to the economy.

The crucial question that should be asked is how many people are taken out of the labor force because of SSDI? In 2014, 3% of America's prime aged men were getting disability insurance compared to only 1% back in 1967. An explanation to this increase could be that millions of prime aged men are applying for the disability insurance in order to attempt sustaining themselves without working. Eberstadt did not hold the government responsible for the increasing number of 'economically inactive' men yet he emphasized on its economic role. He highlighted that in 1960, for every disabled man there were around 134 workers; however, by 2010, the number dropped to just 16. Although the economy has produced around 1.2 million non-farm jobs between 2010 and 2011, nearly half the workers in the field became beneficiaries of the disability allowance. The situation seems to be difficult to understand because with the newly created jobs, the work environment became stress and danger free.

If this explanation turns to be positive, it will only explain a quarter of the number of prime aged men who disappeared from the workforce. Various reasons should push the reformation of the SSDI. However, it is not the sole cause behind the fall of the male participation rate in the labor market.

Stay at Home Fathers

Married men are more inclined towards finding a job than their single men. Fathers are also more likely to work than non-fathers. Moreover, more than three quarters of unemployed prime aged men are not matched with an employed wife. Furthermore, employed men are more likely to be handling household responsibilities than unemployed men.

Eberstadt suggests there is a correlation between job hunting and marriage. The drop of male participation rate in the workforce has been accompanied with the abandonment of marriage. Since 1965, the rate of men who have not been married has tripled; Eberstadt relies on this fact to claim there is a growing infantilization. He also uses the fact that the 'economically inactive' men watch television for 5.5 hours daily which means 2 hours more than the typical men who are unemployed but looking for jobs.

The Prison System

This is by far the most problematic issue of all. There are around 1.1 million American men in prison. They should not, however, affect the number of men forming the workforce as the government removed them from the calculations. Nevertheless, statistics have shown more disturbing facts; around 9 million men have been detained. However, this fact is not the problem. The issue is that, according to the White House economists, after their release they are most likely to fall into unemployment. What is more disturbing is the fact that in a great number of states, men who have been incarcerated are denied the right to take part in a considerable number of jobs.

Therefore, researchers have been tempted to uncover the effects of jail on employment. A research conducted back in 2010 by John Schmitt and Kris Warner at the Center for

Economic and Policy Research (CEPR) on ex-offenders and the labor market has shown that prison could in fact reduce the employment time for a 45 years old man by 19% percent. Furthermore, ex-offenders are less likely to get employed by 30% than men who have not been incarcerated. There are no doubts that having been to jail makes it harder for men to find a decent job. However, even with making the harshest assumptions about the difficulty for ex-offenders to be employed, the number of incarcerated and recently released offenders do not fully explain the fall of male participation rate in the labor force.

Workplace Participation

The participation rate of prime aged men in the workforce has been undeniably affected by the possibilities explained previously. Men disappearing from the workforce might be struggling with job stability or reaching to disability payments in order to flee jobs with poor salaries. They might be continuing their education or even serving as stay at home fathers while having working partners but the latest seem to be less likely to happen.

On one hand, the essence behind the disappearance of prime aged men from the workforce lies in the continuous shrinking of sectors largely dominated by men. Back in 1954, 40% of the jobs were related to the manufacturing and construction sectors and the male participation rate in the workforce was at its peak. Today, only 13% of the jobs are related to the same sectors. The considerable decline in the number of jobs available in the mentioned sectors have affected negatively the participation rate of men without college degree who usually depend on these kinds of jobs to sustain themselves. However, jobs related to construction and manufacturing are harder to find today. According to the report published by the White House economists, prime aged men are more likely to participate in jobs in the field of construction, mining and manufacturing with varying degrees. They are drawn to jobs which are both heavily male-oriented and subsidized by the government.

On the other hand, jobs judged to be female oriented are growing especially in the private sector. In the next decade, jobs like marketing specialists, medical secretaries, home health and personal care aides are predicted to create around 100,000 job opportunities. In all of the areas expected to grow, females have more share than males. Lawrence Katz, a professor of economics in Harvard University, attributes the decline in male participation in the workforce to be a discrepancy between expectation and identity which in fact highlighted by the belief that whoever working as a health technician should be a female. The number of available jobs has significantly increased in fields considered female oriented such as health, education and government.

Plans for Addressing Unemployment in America

The United States of America might be in need for great reform project in order to give idle men jobs they are proud to be doing. However, with Donald Trump's administration in charge, it is expected that manufacturing jobs will remain on hold.

Nevertheless, it seems to be a different story with construction jobs. Conor Sen, a portfolio manager and a columnist at Bloomberg View, predicted that the following five years will witness a boom in the construction sector. What worried Sen is the ability to find enough workers for the expected boom mainly because the construction jobs are considered male oriented jobs in which around more than 90% of the workers are men. Construction jobs are also filled by workers who are young and less educated, and according to Sen, America's population is growing older and more educated. He claims that if construction projects require 500,000 workers they will not be available.

What Sen does not know is that construction workers are available. Millions of men who would like to work in the construction field have left the workforce and stopped looking for a suitable well-paying job. They might be living in areas where the male unemployment rate is around 40% like Appalachia, the Rust Belt, or the Deep South. Moreover, low-cost housing should be installed in rich and crowded metro areas in the United States.

The report published by the White House economists suggests possible means to increase the male participation rate in the workforce. They propose reforming the criminal justice system and removing occupational licenses. They also dared to recommend a plan to transfer men from areas with high unemployment rates for men towards areas with widely available construction jobs. The bold move in this recommendation is that this plan should be depending economically on the state. It should include unprecedented collaboration from different levels of the government. Urban areas should be transformed to allow building low cost housing and GOP Congress should approve a costly plan it has highlighted it will not implement.

Despite the social disturbance that might occur for families and children because of the unexpected dislocation, it might be a necessary disturbance. However, unemployed men are mostly young, single and have no children. Encouraging men who are already disconnected from the economy to relocate in order to provide them with a community and a stable job might be a great idea to bring them back from their alienation.

According to Eberstadt, the welfare reform that took place in 1996 has helped women and especially single mothers to participate in the labor force. Therefore, he suggests further reforms to turn around the social emasculation of 'economically inactive' men. Eberstadt also claims that Donald Trump supporters might be formed of idle men who are angry because of the loss of their self-esteem, masculinity, and purpose.

Physical and Intellectual Labor

Obama's council of economic advisers stated clearly that 83% of prime aged men are out of the labor force and most of them were not working the past year. Nicholas Eberstadt claims the information about men out of the labor force are scarce. They might be single, less educated or black; such factors are not certain. However, the reason behind quitting the job market and the way the spend their abundant free time are still a mystery. Cases of three 'economically inactive' men will be explored to understand their motives and lifestyle leading to abandoning the workforce.

First, Romeo Barnes lives in District Height, MD., and he used to work at Wal-Mart as a greeter 11 years ago. He is a 30 years old single black man with cerebral palsy. Barnes claims that even his perfectly healthy friends cannot find a suitable job which makes it normal for him to be out of the labor force in his opinion. He also admits that he wanted to apply for administrative jobs but his disability and his lack of needed education stood in his way. He believes the jobs that used to be filled with men without a college degree are being replaced with technology.

Barnes' claims are actually supported by professional opinion. Economists state that technology and offshoring are reducing the number of available jobs. According to Bill Gates, the cofounder of Microsoft, the largest PC software company in the world, stresses on the need to tax companies using robots in order to find alternative jobs or provide trainings and education material for employees who are increasingly replaced by the advancements of technology. However, Angus Deaton, a Scottish American economist and winner of Nobel Memorial Prize in Economic Sciences, claims that Gates' proposition is nearly impossible to accomplish because of the inseparable integration between business and technology.

Additionally, men with disabilities are increasingly relying on disability insurance. Nearly, 20 million Americans have been incarcerated and most of them are men; in other words, one out of eight American men has a criminal record. According to Eberstadt, it is hard to know to what extent having been convicted affects their participation rate in workforce because the government does not keep track of their employment status.

Second, forty percent of unemployed women are stay-at-home mothers but it is only the case for 5% of men out of the labor market. Jory Rekkedal is a stay-at-home father, he left his job in the IT field to take care of his daughters. When he quit, he was not planning to hunt for a job any time soon. Jory explains that going back to work is not easy especially in the field of IT where things evolve faster than usual. He worries that he would not have the know-how needed for the job anymore.

Tara Sinclair, the chief economist for the job search website Indeed.com, highlights that jobs requiring able-bodied workers are shrinking and leading the way to intellectual jobs. Unfortunately, this new situation is not favorable to men especially those without a college degree. Sinclair, therefore, questions whether men who quit their jobs might come back provided they get the good opportunities. She stresses that if men continue to remain out of the workforce, the social security will be increasingly burdened as well as the economic growth will slow down.

Last, Richard Hintzke, a 53 years old man, has no children and has relocated to Austin, Texas. Hintzke used to have a property valuation business that shut down after the collapse of the housing market in 2009. He says what he misses the most about his work is the companionship and the feeling of contributing. Hintzke is considering a shift career to holistic wellness. However, he is concerned that he lost the momentum to work because he has been away from work for long.

A Hillbilly Reflects on Unemployment

J.D. Vance, a Yale Law School graduate is currently a spokesperson for the white working class. He grew up in poverty and turmoil. In an interview with The American Conservative, Vance started by saying "These people, my people, are struggling. There has not been a single political candidate who speaks to those struggles for a long time." Vance claims that those who are living the American Dream are hunted by the demons of their past and those who are not are hunted by the demons of depression, neediness and anger.

Vance grew up in an "Ohio steel town" with a great number of jobs and hope. His mother was addicted to drugs and his grandparents who have not graduated from high school are the ones who raised him. According to Vance, based on statistics, people who were raised in a similar situation will mostly face a gloomy future; they end either as heroin addicts or just avoid well-being. However, Vance is one of very few white men who was raised in similar environments and was able to change their destiny. He graduated from Yale Law School, got married, and began working as an executive in Silicon Valley.

Vance's grandparents moved from Kentucky to Ohio in order to find a job in a steel company called Armco. They were together since their teenage years. Vance's grandfather was an alcohol addict while his grandmother was not really a pleasant person. During one fight between his grandparents, his grandmother threatened his grandfather that he would lose his life if he decided to get drunk again. She actually decided to realize her threat with a lighter fluid and a match, but Vance's grandfather survived.

Vance's uncle and aunt left the unhealthy family they were raised in and built stable families both socially and economically. Unlike his mother who continued to suffer from the scars of her childhood. She used to be a top student during high school, but she fell pregnant before graduating. She became a nurse and had very unstable relationships with men. Her lifestyle slowly destroyed her children. Because of her struggle with drugs, her inability to commit to rehab, and losing her nursing license she became a very delinquent and abusive mother. After an intense fight with Vance, he ran to stranger's house fearing that his own mother might kill him.

Although Vance's tragedy with his mother would bring anger and bitterness to anyone who hears it, Vance has different feelings. He sympathized with the pain his mother was feeling and was trying to numb with the drugs, and with the abuse she faced as a child shaping her toxically shamed adult behavior. In his book, Vance always returned to the intense relationship he had with his mother trying to understand the reason why some children surrender to the abuse they have seen, and others survive through their struggles. He questions whether his mother was a victim, an abuser or even both, and whether people can escape their past and their class. Vance left his mother's house when he was in 10th grade to live with a slightly matured grandmother. She helped him endure his school days through buying him the necessary things he needed and encouraging him to work hard and engage in school. She taught him that he only holds the keys to his future. Vance eventually graduated, and he had good grades that could help him enroll in college. However, the financial aid and debt were actually terrifying for both Vance and his grandmother. Therefore, he decided to get enlisted in the Marines where he learned to be disciplined, to manage his time effectively and most importantly to believe in his ability to survive his struggles.

After the military, Vance went to Law School and he had to confront his inherited lifestyle. Vance states that moving from the working class to the professional class highlights that the usual life behaviors become either outdated or unhealthy. Vance summarized his struggles when he said "social mobility is not just about money and economics, it is about lifestyle change". In fact, Vance decided one day to take Yale friends to a restaurant he used to go to with his grandmother on special occasions, but they considered as "a greasy public health crisis".

Vance also fell in an embarrassing situation in which he spat out mineral water because he thought it was bad as he had never tested it before.

Although Vance has faced and overcome his struggles, he still holds compassion for those who are living like he used to. He describes his home as a hub of despair with drug addiction, poverty, low social mobility and divorce. He calls the white working class as the most pessimistic group in America. He considers such pessimism as being the byproduct of social isolation that is passed on from one generation to the other.

Vance stands for the fact the wounds the white working class are facing are partially self-inflicted. From his point of view, they have lost the sense of belonging as well as their appetite for hard work. He willingly writes a story about the time he had to work in a summer job in a local factory. He used to earn $13 per hour with various possibilities for advancement. Vance states that a full-time employee could earn his fair share monthly that could allow him to live a satisfactory life. Although the jobs at the factory were well paying jobs, the factory owner found it was a difficult task to fill the available jobs. During Vance's time at the factory, three employees quit their jobs. Additionally, a 19 years old man named Bob has been fired for being usually late and taking long bathroom breaks. Bob had a pregnant girlfriend. When Bob got fired, he out bursted with anger against his manager refusing to take responsibility of his actions. Vance understood the feelings of Bob who thought he was the subject of the factory's poor management. He felt like he does not have the ability to control his own life. He blamed everyone except himself.

Vance's key to success can therefore be drawn out of Bob's story. Vance pushed through his difficult times instead of giving up or blaming everyone. Vance is surely proud of being hillbilly. However, he questions whether hillbillies are tough enough to face themselves and recognize that their behavior is destroying their children. Public policy, according to Vance, is necessary but it is not enough because he claims that white working men should stop blaming the government or forgettable companies for their problems and start actually asking themselves what they could do to make things better. Nevertheless, Angus Deaton explains that representatives of working class have disappeared from Congress and trade unions are slowly dying and losing their political stamina. Therefore, policies are needed to help the working-class hillbillies become economically active and connect with the American society.

Being Unemployed in America Compared to the Third World

Angus Deaton studies philosophical questions rather than just pure economics. He wonders whether the world is getting better or worse, whether inequality is increasing or decreasing, what makes people happy and how welfare should be measured. According to the Nobel Laureate and retired Princeton economist, the world is certainly getting better but not everywhere and not for everyone. In a conference held by the National Association of Business Economics, Deaton mentioned inequality among countries is shrinking; however, inequality between social classes in countries is augmenting. He proved his point of view with the visible boost of India and China's economic status as well as the slightly increasing economic gain some African sub-Saharan countries are attaining. However, within countries, the richer is getting richer while the middle class is increasingly suffering deprivation.

Because of the United Nations' Sustainable Development Goals (SDG), the World Bank is now collecting income number in developed and developing countries. Surprisingly, Deaton believes that living in World Bank's poorest countries might better than living in the United States. Deaton cites $2.00 a day, a book by authored by Luke Shaefer and Kathy Edin, and Evicted, a book by Matthew Desmond to stress on the fact there are 3 million American men living under poverty line.

Although the infrastructure in America such as health care, roads, education system and development programs are among the benefits of living there, Deaton claims that expectation of life in areas in America like Appalachia is lower than the expectation of life in Bangladesh. The millions of dollars spent on Medicaid as well as the infrastructure are surely valuable but the question raised by Deaton is how to measure such services. In fact, feeding children or finding a place to live in cannot be done through the millions of Medicaid. The idea Deaton trying to sell is even though poverty is complicated and countries comparisons might not be fair, people might choose to live in a poor town in India rather than Mississippi Delta.

Moreover, Deaton met a great number of Montana residents who are absolutely anti-government. He states how they view the government with this anecdote "that wolf is eating my cow and I need to get a bureaucrat on the line before I'm allowed to shoot it! And that's my year's income!" In other words, the government has been granting lands to farmers in Montana and that has been destroying their lives since it was nearly impossible to turn the lands into actual farms. Therefore, they cannot put their hopes unto government's help. Deaton explains the government enforces equality because of the redistribution of wealth; however, it also helps inequality because of the continuous situation of cronyism.

Poverty and Illegal Drugs

The claim Deaton has made about the middle class is also valid for the United States and it is actually supported by a study he conducted with famous Princeton economist Anne Case. In their study, they reached a disturbing conclusion; mortality is hunting middle-aged white men and it is caused by overdose and suicide. They named it "deaths of despair". Deaton explains that opioid and OxyContin should be discussed by the government to stop or even limit the overdose deaths. Opioid is dangerous because if the drug addict relapses he is risking his life unlike alcohol and other drugs. However, there are foggy discussions about opioid is not prescribed for men with color on purpose and whether there are some kind of division in addiction.

Deaton highlights the deaths caused by OxyContin are deaths caused by rent-seeking and cronyism. He stresses the fact there are two kinds of drug dealers and there is one that is selling drugs under the license of the American government. The less fortunate people who do not have access to Medicaid are for the majority addicted to the OxyContin drug. OxyContin addiction has gone beyond control; it is unbelievably heartbreaking to find out there is a town in Indiana that has given up money and uses grams OxyContin as a currency. The disturbing fact that although people became highly dependent on OxyContin there are enough prescribed for everyone. Dependence on government has been given a whole new meaning according to Eberstadt. If people addicted to OxyContin could get medical prescription to use the drug it will be financed Medicaid if the addicts are insured. Deaton explains that the beneficiaries of the Medicaid are not people who are consuming OxyContin because they are consuming and dying. However, the real beneficiaries are the ones behind the creation of the addictive drug. The Food and Drug Administration (FDA) works in the favor of pharmaceutical companies rather than the American citizens. According to George Stigler, a Nobel Prize

Laureate in Economics, one of the worst threats to regulation is when it gets manipulated by those it should regulate. It is clearly the case with the FDA and OxyContin approvals. The FDA could limit its use to hospitals like in Britain.

The decreasing participation rate of men in the labor market has discovered problems in various areas from pharmaceutical rent-seeking to SSDI needed reforms. However, unemployed men are the ones who are suffering even though with all the discussions. Clear and fast actions to help the community and the individuals are highly needed.

Thanks for Reading

Hello, this message is from Naven Johnson. I hope that you enjoyed this book and that it has helped your life in some way. It is my intention to create information that readers will find useful and valuable.

I am grateful when people read books and I are even more grateful when my readers leave a review. Please leave a review that lets me know what you liked about this book so that I can work on improving future books.